REPUBLIC OF KOREA 2016 HUMAN RIGHTS REPORT

Note: This report was updated 3/03/17; see Appendix F: Errata for more information.

EXECUTIVE SUMMARY

The Republic of Korea (South Korea) is a constitutional democracy governed by a president and a unicameral legislature. Observers considered parliamentary general elections during the year and presidential elections in 2012 free and fair.

Civilian authorities maintained effective control over security forces.

The primary human rights problems reported were government interpretation and application of the National Security Law, libel laws, and other laws to limit freedom of speech and expression and restrict internet access; and the continued jailing of conscientious objectors to military service. Corruption was also a problem. Choi Soon-sil, a long-time friend and close confidante of President Park Geun-hye, was arrested and indicted on charges of fraud, coercion, and abuse of power. She was accused of amassing a personal fortune by using her personal ties to Park, and the president's knowledge of or involvement in Choi's activities is under investigation. In light of the scandal, lawmakers voted 234-56 to impeach President Park in December. Meanwhile, thousands of anti-Park demonstrators took to the streets in massive but peaceful rallies held on consecutive Saturdays for several weeks.

Other human rights problems included the absence of a comprehensive anti-discrimination law, sexual and domestic violence, and trafficking in persons including sex trafficking of children. Societal discrimination occurred against defectors from the Democratic People's Republic of Korea (North Korea or DPRK); ethnic/racial minorities; lesbian, gay, bisexual, transgender, and intersex (LGBTI) persons; persons with HIV/AIDS; and foreigners. Restrictions on workers' rights, including freedom of association and assembly and limitations on political engagement of public servants and teachers, were also problematic.

The government took steps to prosecute officials who committed abuses, and impunity was not evident.

Section 1. Respect for the Integrity of the Person, Including Freedom from:

a. Arbitrary Deprivation of Life and other Unlawful or Politically Motivated Killings

Reported suicides among military personnel increased slightly to 27 during the first half of the year, compared to 24 during the same period in 2015. Efforts by the Ministry of National Defense (MND) to address institutional deficiencies that contributed to a high rate of killings and suicides among recruits led to some improvements, and MND reported an overall decrease in the number of deaths in the past three years. Suicides were generally attributed to bullying, hazing, or inability to adjust to military life.

b. Disappearance

There were no reports of politically motivated disappearances.

c. Torture and Other Cruel, Inhuman, or Degrading Treatment or Punishment

The law prohibits such practices, although there were credible reports that government officials employed them during the year.

As in 2015, MND reported no instances of bullying in the military despite the general belief that hazing played a role in suicides in the military (see section 1.a.). Despite the apparent elimination of bullying and hazing in the military, credible evidence indicated mistreatment of soldiers persisted. The Military Human Rights Center reported 245 cases of bullying and hazing filed between January and September.

Since the MND established a Human Rights Evaluation System in 2014, its military human rights monitors received approximately 380 proposals to improve human rights in the military as of July. To address these suggestions, the MND implemented the Basic Law for the Status and Service of Military Personnel in June. The law aims to ensure the basic rights of personnel and provide remedies for violations of human rights. With support from the National Human Rights Commission of Korea, the MND trained approximately 600 military human rights instructors per year and aimed to have 3,000 trained instructors by 2019.

Prison and Detention Center Conditions

Prison and detention center conditions generally met international standards.

An Airlines Operators Committee, consisting of 60 member airlines, funded and staffed a "departure waiting area" inside Incheon International Airport for travelers denied entry to the country, including migrants and asylum seekers. The Ministry of Justice (MOJ) is the managing government authority responsible for the area.

Persons in the area may contact a lawyer and appeal their denial of entry. Twenty-eight Syrian asylum seekers lived in the area from December 2015 to July 2016. A Nigerian asylum seeker had been in the area for more than 10 months as of September. On average, 108 persons stayed in the area daily between January and June, according to the MOJ. The departure waiting area had the capacity to accommodate approximately 60 persons.

The Ministry asserted the area was equipped with beds, shower stalls, televisions, and public telephones, and approximately half of all occupants returned to their respective countries the same day they were denied entry. International organizations and NGOs operating in the country , however, described living conditions in the waiting room as substandard--lacking privacy, bedding, and medical care--especially for those confined to the room for several months. Occupants depended on their respective airlines for food. Some received fast-food meals three times a day, while others received nothing and relied on other travelers or their asylum lawyers for sustenance.

Physical Conditions: Deaths in prison were generally consistent with death rates/causes nationally.

Administration: Authorities investigated credible allegations of problematic conditions and documented the results of such investigations in a publicly accessible manner.

Independent Monitoring: There were no problems reported with access to prison facilities. The country's independent National Human Rights Commission has access to correctional facilities to investigate reported cases of human rights violations. The International Committee of the Red Cross did not request monitoring of detention conditions during the year.

d. Arbitrary Arrest or Detention

The law prohibits arbitrary arrest and detention, and the government generally observed these prohibitions.

The National Security Law (NSL) grants authorities the power to detain, arrest, and imprison persons believed to have committed acts intended to endanger the "security of the state." Domestic and international nongovernmental organizations (NGOs) continued to call for reform or repeal of the law, contending its provisions do not clearly define prohibited activity. Amnesty International's 2015/16 report stated the government expanded NSL application to include new categories of violations and additional groups of individuals, such as foreign nationals.

Role of the Police and Security Apparatus

The Korean National Police Agency (KNPA) is responsible for internal security under the supervision of the Ministry of the Interior (formerly the Ministry of Government Administration and Home Affairs). The Korean Immigration Service is responsible for migration and border enforcement under the supervision of the Ministry of Justice. Civilian authorities maintained effective control over police, and the government had effective mechanisms to investigate and punish abuse and corruption.

The National Intelligence Service (NIS) has the authority to investigate crimes or criminal activity related to national security and subversion. Civil society organizations continued to claim that extensive NIS powers and secrecy combined with little oversight enabled the NIS unreasonably and expansively to define and investigate activities it deemed a threat to national security.

According to the KNPA, there were no reports of impunity involving security forces during the year. Some NGOs and worker's rights groups commented the removal of name tags from uniforms worn by police mobilized to manage protests raised questions about impunity, particularly when forceful suppression techniques--such as water cannons--were used against individual protesters.

Arrest Procedures and Treatment of Detainees

The law requires warrants in cases of arrest, detention, seizure, or search, except if authorities apprehend a person while committing a criminal act, if a judge is not available, or if authorities believe a suspect may destroy evidence or escape capture if not arrested quickly. In such cases, a public prosecutor or police officer must prepare an affidavit of emergency arrest immediately upon apprehension of the suspect. Authorities may not interrogate for more than six hours a person who voluntarily submits to questioning at a police station. Authorities must either indict or release an arrested suspect within 20 days. The law allows 10 additional days of detention in exceptional circumstances.

There is a bail system. Human rights lawyers stated authorities generally did not grant bail for detainees who were charged with committing serious offenses, may attempt to flee or harm another individual, or had no fixed address.

The law provides for the right to representation by an attorney, including during police interrogation. There were no reports of denial of access to counsel. There are no restrictions on access to a lawyer, but authorities can limit a lawyer's participation in an interrogation if the lawyer obstructs the interrogation or discloses information that impedes an investigation. During the trial stage, and under certain circumstances during the pretrial stage, an indigent detainee may request that the government provide a lawyer.

Access to family members during detention varied according to the severity of the crime.

Arbitrary Arrest: The Ministry of Justice reported 10 arrests between January and June for violating the NSL. All 10 suspects were indicted on criminal charges.

In September the Seoul High Court ruled charges brought against Yoo Woo-sung for violating the Foreign Exchange Transactions Act were a "retaliatory indictment" by prosecutors. Yoo's alleged violation consisted of assisting North Korean defectors in the country to remit funds to family members in the DPRK. He was previously indicted on charges of espionage under the National Security Law but was acquitted in October 2015 after the discovery that National Intelligence Service staff had forged evidence against him. The High Court's ruling acknowledged that prosecutors were pressing charges in retaliation for the forgery scandal.

Detainee's Ability to Challenge Lawfulness of Detention before a Court: Criminal suspects have the right to petition the court for habeas corpus.

e. Denial of Fair Public Trial

The law provides for an independent judiciary, and the government generally respected judicial independence.

Trial Procedures

The constitution provides for the right to a fair public trial, and an independent judiciary generally enforced this right. By law defendants in criminal trials are presumed innocent and enjoy protection against self-incrimination and have the right to be informed promptly and in detail of charges, with free interpretation as necessary; to communicate with an attorney (at public expense if necessary); to have a fair and speedy trial; to attend the trial; and to appeal. Defendants received adequate time and facilities to prepare a defense. They are also protected against retroactive laws and double jeopardy, although prosecutors can appeal not-guilty verdicts. Initial trials must begin within six months of arrest.

Trials are open to the public, but judges may restrict attendance if they believe spectators might disrupt the proceedings. There is a jury system, but jury verdicts are not legally binding. In serious cases such as murder and rape, the judge may consent to a legally binding jury verdict, provided it is reached in consultation with the judge. The defendant must request a jury trial beforehand.

Judges have considerable scope to examine witnesses for both the prosecution and defense. Defendants may not be compelled to testify or confess guilt and may have access to relevant government-held evidence.

Political Prisoners and Detainees

The Ministry of Justice stated there were no persons incarcerated solely because of their political beliefs. Some NGOs, however, argued that individuals arrested for violations of the NSL, for conscientious objection to military service, or for strike activities qualified as political prisoners.

The law requires military service by all male citizens and does not distinguish conscientious objectors from others who do not report for duty; the penalty for failing or refusing to report is up to three years in prison. There is no provision for alternative service by conscientious objectors, although the MND may grant exemptions for health, disability, or other reasons. The NGO Watchtower stated that, between January and July, 400 Jehovah's Witnesses were imprisoned for failure to report for duty. Amnesty International reported there were 499 persons in prison for conscientious objection as of July, including persons detained in previous years.

Civil Judicial Procedures and Remedies

There is an independent and impartial judiciary in civil matters, and there were no problems enforcing domestic court orders. Citizens had court access to bring lawsuits seeking damages for, or cessation of, a human rights violation. Individuals and organizations may appeal adverse decisions to domestic human rights bodies, and then to the UN Human Rights Committee. Administrative and judicial remedies are available for alleged wrongs.

f. Arbitrary or Unlawful Interference with Privacy, Family, Home, or Correspondence

The law prohibits such actions, and the government generally respected these prohibitions. The law establishes conditions under which the government may monitor telephone calls, mail, and other forms of communication for up to two months in criminal investigations and four months in national security cases. The Security Surveillance Act requires some persons sentenced to prison for breaching the NSL to report their whereabouts, travel plans, family relations, occupation, and financial status to a local police office within seven days of leaving prison and every third month thereafter.

The NSL forbids citizens from listening to DPRK radio programs in their homes or reading books published in the DPRK if the government determines such an action endangers national security or the basic order of democracy. Enforcement of these prohibitions continued to be rare, however, and viewing DPRK satellite telecasts in private homes is legal.

In March lawmakers passed a controversial Counterterrorism Act that had been stalled in the National Assembly since it was first proposed 15 years ago. The act aims to protect the country against terrorist attacks and North Korean espionage. Opposition party lawmakers and NGOs, however, claimed it significantly expands NIS power to wiretap civilians' telephones and collect personal information. Thirty-eight opposition lawmakers filibustered the bill for 10 hours, saying it would allow the NIS to monitor not only suspected terrorists but also critics of the administration, particularly online.

Section 2. Respect for Civil Liberties, Including:

a. Freedom of Speech and Press

The law provides for freedom of speech and press. Nonetheless, the government's interpretation of the following limited freedom of speech and expression and restricted access to the internet: the NSL; Article 21, Paragraph 4 of the constitution; the Act on Antiterrorism for the Protection of Citizens and Public Security; the Election Law; the Criminal Act; the Framework Act on Telecommunications (Framework Act); and the Act on Promotion of Information and Communication Network Utilization and Information Protection (Network Act).

<u>Freedom of Speech and Expression</u>: Although the law provides for freedom of speech, under laws such as the NSL the government may limit the expression of ideas that praise or incite the activities of "anti-state" individuals or groups. During the year, prosecutions under the NSL for speech that allegedly supported or praised the DPRK government continued. Individuals whom authorities deem to have criticized the country's political leaders may be punished under laws that criminalize defamation, whether fact-based or false, if the comments are deemed not to be in the public interest.

Human Rights Watch claimed the government undermined the free exchange of opinions that are fundamental to democracy. Amnesty International's 2015/16 report stated the government increasingly restricted freedom of expression by using the NSL to intimidate and imprison individuals.

In May the Seoul Central District Court found foreign citizen Shin Eun-mi not guilty of violating the NSL for making comments considered complimentary of North Korea. In July, however, the Seoul Administrative Court upheld the government's January 2015 decision to deport Shin. A five-year ban on Shin's return remained in place.

Under the election law, the government can limit the expression of ideas that the National Election Commission deems to be false. In March, ahead of the April General Elections, a blogger's post criticizing ruling party Representative Na Kyung-won was removed less than 10 hours after it was uploaded. His post called for Na to respond to a viral news story alleging her daughter had received preferential treatment in a college admissions process for students with disabilities. Through the blog operator Kakao, the National Election Commission notified him of the removal of the post because it spread false information about political candidates. Under the law, companies receive fines if they do not implement the election commission's removal requests. Following the removal of his post, the police summoned the police every day for a week to be questioned about a factual mistake in his post. The blogger ignored the summons and the commission eventually dropped the case without pressing charges, but NGOs noted the election law's chilling effect on freedom of expression.

<u>Press and Media Freedoms</u>: Independent media were active and expressed a wide variety of views, but strict defamation laws limited freedom of the press. The UN Special Rapporteur on the promotion and protection of the right to freedom of opinion and expression voiced concern that defamation suits, filed for statements that were true and in the public interest, penalized individuals who criticized the government. The NGO Reporters Without Borders significantly downgraded the country's press freedom ranking, in large part because of the increasingly poor relationship between the government and media rather than because of legal or regulatory changes.

<u>Censorship or Content Restrictions</u>: The Ministry of Gender Equality and Family monitors song lyrics and may ban releases it considers offensive. The Korea Communications Standards Commission (KCSC) maintains ethical standards in broadcasting and internet communications. The UN Special Rapporteur on freedom of expression and opinion previously expressed concerns about insufficient safeguards to ensure the KCSC does not operate as a de facto censorship body to delete content critical of the government or powerful corporations.

The Ministry of Education created a taskforce in November 2015 to push ahead with plans to require middle and high schools to use only Korean history books authored by the government-affiliated National Institute of Korean History starting in March 2017. This would end the right of schools, since 2010, to choose from a range of textbooks approved by the ministry. In coordination with the main opposition party, lawyers representing civil society groups filed an injunction with the Constitutional Court in July to block the ministry's plan. Similar injunctions were filed with the Seoul Administrative Court in January. The courts were reviewing the cases and had not announced a decision. In November the Ministry of Education published a preliminary version of the government-authored history textbook online to collect public feedback for one month. The government's decision to require real name verification for submitting feedback and to block public access to submitted comments caused further controversy. In December the ministry announced that it will no longer mandate the use of state-authored textbooks. They will be released in March 2018, a year later than planned, should some schools wish to use them.

<u>Libel/Slander Laws</u>: The government and individual public figures used the law, which broadly defines and criminalizes defamation, to restrict public discussion and harass, intimidate, or censor private and media expression. The law allows punishment of up to three years in prison for true comments and up to seven years for statements considered false. The law punishes defamation of deceased persons as well; the maximum punishment is two year's imprisonment.

Attempts to amend defamation laws were largely unsuccessful. In February the Constitutional Court ruled against a proposal to ban defamation charges in cases when a comment circulated online is true.

<u>National Security</u>: The NSL criminalizes actions interpreted to be in support of North Korea or otherwise against the state. The government used this law to arrest and imprison civilians, deport foreigners, and disband political parties. The Supreme Court ruled the NSL constitutional in 2015.

Internet Freedom

There were some government restrictions on internet access, and the government monitored e-mail and internet chat rooms with wide authority under the law. Internet access was available and used widely.

The KCSC determines whether posts made on social networking sites, such as Twitter and Facebook, or in chat rooms contain unlawful content, defined as harmful or illegal speech. If the government finds prohibited materials, it has the authority to warn the user. If the prohibited materials are not removed, the user's account may be blocked. In addition, a taskforce in the Seoul Central District Prosecutor's Office monitored the internet for false information and removed it when discovered.

The government blocked violent, sexually explicit, gambling-oriented, and other websites found to violate law and order, including, but not limited to, the illegal trade of internal organs, food, or medical supplies; violation of intellectual property rights; and the encouragement or planning of suicide. The government continued to block DPRK websites and direct access to the DPRK's YouTube channel and Twitter account. Although viewing websites praising the DPRK regime is lawful, disseminating information about those websites, including posting links to the sites, is unlawful under the NSL.

During the first of half of the year, the KCSC blocked content promoting the DPRK regime and Juche ideology on Facebook and Twitter accounts believed to be operated by DPRK cyber agents. In March the KCSC blocked access to North Korea Tech, a foreign-based blog about information technology in the DPRK. The National Intelligence Service asserted three articles on the blog violated the NSL. Local civil society groups filed an appeal but three of the five voting members of the commission voted against it in May.

Although the requirement that persons use their real names when making online postings to large websites was ruled unconstitutional in 2012, the election campaign law requires real names for internet postings about forthcoming elections (see section 3).

In March the Open Government Partnership reported concerns about the government's commitment to open governance and urged it to address fundamental issues such as corruption and online access to information by citizens. Freedom House assessed the country's internet and press as "partly free."

Academic Freedom and Cultural Events

There were no government restrictions specifically targeting academic freedom or cultural events. In December the government cancelled plans to require middle and high schools to use state-authored Korean history textbooks (see above).

In May a Seoul court permitted a theater owned by the state broadcaster (Korean Broadcasting System) to cancel four shows by the Shen Yun performing arts company. The decision reversed a ruling by the same court in April. Shen Yun is associated with China's banned Falun Gong movement. The theater acted after it received a letter from the Chinese embassy; the court ruling appeared to be based on the potential "huge losses" to the broadcaster (one of few foreign media outlets allowed to broadcast in China) should China revoke its broadcast rights there.

b. Freedom of Peaceful Assembly and Association

Freedom of Assembly

The law provides for freedom of assembly, and the government generally respected this right. The Assembly and Demonstrations Act prohibits or places limitations on assemblies considered likely to undermine public order and requires notification of police in advance of demonstrations of all types, including political rallies. Police must notify organizers if they consider an event impermissible under this law. Police banned some protests by groups that had not properly registered or that were responsible for violent protests in the past. Police also banned nine assemblies in the first half of the year because two or more assembly applications were submitted for the same place. Some NGOs suggested companies work through pro-employer "yellow" unions to submit assembly applications in advance and thereby prevent other groups from protesting near the company building. The KNPA reported 38 of more than 10,000 assembly applications received through June were denied or conditionally limited. Some NGOs contended that Article 314 of the Criminal Act, regarding obstruction of business, restricts the right to peaceful assembly.

Local and international observers questioned the tactics and technology used by the KNPA to manage large-scale protests. For example, much of the violence at a November 2015 "People's Rally" (see section 7.a.) surrounded a barricade of hundreds of buses parked bumper to bumper completely blocking off access to streets. Protesters sought to break through or knock over the bus barricade, and physical clashes between the KNPA and the protesters ensued. Baek Nam-gi, an elderly protester hit by a water cannon at the rally, was in a coma for many months following the incident, dying in September. No charges were filed against the KNPA operator of the water cannon, and civil society groups called on the government to issue a formal apology and investigate the circumstances surrounding Baek's death. In response, the KNPA applied for a warrant to perform an autopsy on Baek, but family opposition had blocked the effort as of November.

The June 15 "Report of the UN Special Rapporteur on the rights to freedom of peaceful assembly and of association on his mission to the Republic of Korea" stated that the use of police bus barricades "triggers increased tensions" and that these barricades were "not used reactively to manage the conduct of participants, but rather pre-emptively to interfere with the right to freedom of peaceful assembly."

Police arrested 22 labor unionists in the aftermath of 2015 protests and the president of the Korean Confederation of Trade Unions was sentenced to five years in prison in July. All 22 unionists were indicted; six were still detained at the Seoul Detention Center as of October (see section 7.a.). On his visit to the country in January, the UN Special Rapporteur on the rights to freedom of peaceful assembly and of association expressed his concern about "a trend of gradual regression on the rights to freedom of peaceful assembly and of association."

In the series of protests that drew unprecedented numbers of participants in November against President Park (see section 4), the Seoul Administrative Court ruled in favor of allowing protesters to march toward the Blue House. For the first time in the country's history, protesters were permitted to march on Yulgok Street, a major road within 0.6 miles of the Blue House.

Freedom of Association

The law provides for freedom of association, and the government generally respected this right.

c. Freedom of Religion

See the Department of State's *International Religious Freedom Report* at www.state.gov/religiousfreedomreport/.

d. Freedom of Movement, Internally Displaced Persons, Protection of Refugees, and Stateless Persons

The law provides for freedom of internal movement, foreign travel (excepting to North Korea), emigration, and repatriation; the government generally respected these rights. The government cooperated with UNHCR and other humanitarian organizations in providing protection and assistance to internally displaced persons, refugees, returning refugees, asylum seekers, stateless persons, and other persons of concern.

Abuse of Migrants, Refugees, and Stateless Persons: According to the Office of the High Commissioner for Human Rights (OHCHR) in Seoul, approximately 70 percent of all defectors from North Korea were women, and many were victims of sexual violence and sex trafficking before and after arriving in South Korea. Recent defectors interviewed by the OHCHR said they expected these crimes as an inevitable part of the defection experience.

Foreign Travel: Citizens traveling to North Korea must obtain permission from the Ministry of Unification before departure. The travelers must demonstrate their trip has no political purpose and is not intended to praise North Korea or criticize the government. Visiting North Korea without government approval is punishable by up to 10 years in prison under the NSL.

The Ministry of Foreign Affairs may limit or revoke passport privileges for citizens indicted for a crime for which the potential sentence is two years' imprisonment or more and citizens convicted of a crime with suspended sentences that have yet to be fulfilled.

Protection of Refugees

<u>Access to Asylum</u>: The law provides for granting asylum or refugee status.

The government considers refugees from North Korea under a separate legal framework and does not include refugees from North Korea in refugee or asylum statistics. The government continued its longstanding policy of accepting refugees or defectors from North Korea, who by law are entitled to South Korean citizenship. The government resettled approximately 894 such persons through August, an increase of 15 percent over the same period in 2015. There were approximately 30,000 registered North Koreans living in the country.

The government operated refugee application counters at airports and harbors to allow asylum seekers to file applications for refugee status upon entering the country. The immigration office at these airports and harbors reviews applications and determines if a case is eligible to be forwarded for refugee status review. It protects asylum seekers' right to an attorney and bans forced repatriation. Asylum seekers can ask for interpretation and legal aid services from the government and receive a work permit six months after application submission.

Requests for asylum continued to increase; 6,041 persons filed for asylum as of October, an increase from the 5,711 applications in all of 2015.

The Ministry of Justice reported that of 18,854 refugee status applicants since 1994, the country granted refugee status to approximately 3 percent (598). The ministry contended many applicants were unable to provide necessary documentation and thus did not qualify for refugee status.

NGOs pointed to understaffing and lack of human resources as major roadblocks to executing a functional refugee and asylum system to handle the sharp increases in asylum applications. As of June, there were 14 refugee officers at the Seoul immigration office and one each at the nine field offices.

<u>Safe Country of Origin/Transit</u>: The law provides grounds on which an asylum seeker at a port of entry may be denied referral for full asylum procedures. These

include arrival "from a safe country of origin or a safe third country, in which little possibility of persecution exists."

In December 2015, this was one of the primary reasons why 28 Syrian applicants (see Section 1.c.) were denied referral to asylum procedures at Incheon International Airport. They traveled through various third countries before their arrival, including China, Lebanon, and Turkey. Over the next several months, with the help of South Korean refugee lawyers, the Syrians disputed the decision and in June the Incheon District Court ruled in favor of the 28 and authorities released 26 of the Syrians from the airport.

<u>Refoulement</u>: Groups working with asylum seekers alleged that in some cases the government might have violated nonrefoulement principles outlined in the UN Convention on Refugees when immigration officers refused applications during "pre-assessment" at the point of entry.

<u>Access to Basic Services</u>: Cultural and social differences posed adjustment difficulties, and many migrants from North Korea and asylum seekers from other countries alleged societal discrimination. These cases were often under-reported, and the National Human Rights Commission reported one discrimination case against an asylum seeker and no formal discrimination cases related to North Korean defectors through September.

<u>Durable Solutions</u>: Through a pilot program that began in 2015, the Ministry of Justice is permanently resettling up to approximately 30 Karen refugees from Myanmar in South Korea annually through 2017. The program was the country's first to resettle foreign refugees, and it provides Korean language classes, social and cultural adjustment education, work-study programs, and counseling services at an immigration reception center near Incheon Airport. The first group of 22 Karen refugees arrived in 2015; the second group of 34 entered the country in November.

<u>Temporary Protection</u>: Government guidelines offer both temporary refugee status in the case of a mass influx of asylum seekers and an alternate form of protection-- a renewable, short-term permit under "humanitarian refugee status"--to those for whom the category of refugee does not apply but for whom there are reasonable grounds to believe their life or personal freedom may be egregiously violated by torture or other problematic treatment or punishment. Of 18,854 refugee status applicants since 1994, 955 individuals received humanitarian refugee status. At year's end approximately 4,750 applications were under review. Regulations

require a refugee status determination within six months of application, but the Justice Ministry's Refugee Division said staffing shortfalls following a nearly 300 percent increase in applications after passage of the 2013 refugee law contributed to an average of 16 months to process an application. The government maintains an immigration reception center where asylum seekers can stay for up to six months while their applications or appeals are processed. Thirty-six individuals were admitted to the immigration reception center in the first half of the year.

In recognition of the humanitarian crisis in Syria, the government decided in 2014 to permit Syrians to stay with humanitarian refugee status without having to go through the usual refugee determination process, which can take years. The Ministry of Justice reported approximately 92 Syrians sought asylum as of June. Of the 955 humanitarian status holders in the country, the majority were Syrians. Others included Palestinians, Egyptians, Chinese, and some Burmese.

Stateless Persons

The Ministry of Justice reported 175 recognized stateless persons as of June. Many were individuals who retained their foreign citizenship after naturalization. As the law did not permit dual citizenship, these individuals lose Korean citizenship and are temporarily stateless in the interim between abandoning their previous nationality and regaining their Korean citizenship. Others enter the country using travel documents for stateless persons, while some naturalized citizens become stateless after losing their Korean citizenship on charges of fraudulent marriages or forged documents.

Children born to North Korean defectors in China were often undocumented and stateless, neither recognized as Chinese citizens nor DPRK defectors. While they can eventually obtain citizenship and may have access to education in defector-oriented schools, the children are not eligible to receive the financial benefits that accompany official defector status. As a result, many defectors choose to leave their stateless children behind in China, where they are particularly vulnerable to abuse and exploitation.

Parents who are undocumented foreign workers often do not register their children with either local authorities or home country embassies for fear of deportation. One local NGO observer estimated there could be 2,000-3,000 such children in the country.

Section 3. Freedom to Participate in the Political Process

The law provides citizens the ability to choose their government in free and fair periodic elections held by secret ballot and based on universal and equal suffrage.

Elections and Political Participation

Recent Elections: Observers generally viewed the 20th National Assembly general elections and by-elections in April and presidential elections in 2012 as free and fair.

In June the Seoul Metropolitan Police Agency seized and searched offices and residences affiliated with the Citizens' Network for the General Election of 2016 (Change 2016) and one of its constituent organizations, People's Solidarity for Participatory Democracy, for allegedly violating election laws. The raids followed a complaint filed by the National Election Commission (NEC) that Change 2016 violated the Public Official Election Act by campaigning against certain lawmakers and conducting a survey without prior notice to the NEC, which it maintains is required by law. Change 2016 used the survey to publish a list of the "10 worst candidates" online. In August the police summoned 22 individuals who participated in Change 2016 activities for questioning. All were indicted in October and were awaiting trial as of November.

Political Parties and Political Participation: Although persons may generally use an alias when making online postings to large websites, the election campaign law requires real names for internet postings about forthcoming elections. Civil society groups called on the National Assembly to repeal that section of the election campaign law as well as a section that bans criticism of individual political candidates, asserting that such laws prohibit the electorate from being freely able to express views, impart information, and campaign.

Participation of Women and Minorities: No laws prevent women or members of minorities from voting, running for office, serving as electoral monitors, or otherwise participating in political life. After Filipina-Korean lawmaker Jasmine Lee lost her seat in the April general elections, there were no nonethnic Korean politicians in office.

Section 4. Corruption and Lack of Transparency in Government

The law provides criminal penalties for official corruption, and the government generally implemented the law effectively; nonetheless, officials sometimes engaged in corrupt practices with impunity and there were numerous reports of government corruption during the year.

In September the Improper Solicitation and Graft Act came into force. It prohibits public servants, teachers, and media from being treated to meals worth more than 30,000 won ($26) or accepting gifts of more than 50,000 won ($43). It was viewed by many as the most stringent anticorruption measure taken by the government in recent years.

Corruption: The Ministry of Justice reported 641 bribery cases involving public officials between January and August 2015. During the year, five lawmakers from the main opposition and ruling parties were charged with receiving bribes or illegal campaign funding.

In July, Jin Kyung-joon became the most senior prosecutor to be indicted in the country's history after allegedly receiving more than 950 million ($818,300) in cash and shares from Kim Jung-ju, the founder of Nexon, the country's largest online gaming company. Jin allegedly received money for family vacations and a luxury sedan from Kim, and he closed a tax investigation against Korean Air after the airline awarded a lucrative contract to his brother-in-law's cleaning company. Jin was dismissed from his position, and if found guilty, faced more than 10 years in prison and fines of up to five times the amount of bribes he received.

Choi Soon-sil, a longtime friend and close confidante of President Park Geun-hye, was arrested and indicted in November on charges of fraud, coercion, and abuse of power. Choi was accused of amassing a personal fortune by using her personal ties to the president to coerce companies to pay tens of millions of dollars to her nonprofit foundations. President Park's former senior secretary for policy coordination, Ahn Jong-beom, was also indicted in November on similar charges for allegedly helping Choi. There was a widespread belief, which led to massive protests (see section 2.b. "Freedom of Assembly") that President Park was implicated in her friend's and associate's activities; the president's knowledge of or involvement in them was under investigation. In light of the scandal, lawmakers voted 234-56, with six abstentions, to impeach President Park in December. Prosecutorial investigations and an official review of Park's impeachment case at the Constitutional Court were to begin in January 2017.

Financial Disclosure: By law public servants above a specified rank, including elected officials, must publicly declare their income and assets, including how they accumulated them. Failure to disclose assets fully is punishable with up to one year in prison and a 10 million won ($8,613) fine.

Corruption allegations in July against Woo Byung-woo, the Senior Presidential Secretary for Civil Affairs, led to a formal police investigation for understating individual and family assets, in violation of the law. He was also under investigation for allegedly using his wife's company to evade taxes and for using his position to secure special treatment for his son during his mandatory military service. Woo resigned in October with eight other high-level aides amid a domestic scandal surrounding President Park Geun-hye and her confidantes.

Public Access to Information: The country has a freedom of information law, and the law was effectively implemented.

Section 5. Governmental Attitude Regarding International and Nongovernmental Investigation of Alleged Violations of Human Rights

A wide variety of domestic and international human rights groups generally operated without government restriction, investigating and publishing their findings on human rights cases. Government officials were somewhat cooperative and responsive to their views. Several large civil society groups, NGOs, and umbrella labor unions claimed that the government restricted their operations or suppressed criticism (see sections 3, "Elections and Political Participation" and 7.a.).

Government Human Rights Bodies: The National Human Rights Commission (NHRC), established as an independent government body to protect and promote the human rights enumerated in the constitution, does not have enforcement power, and its recommendations and decisions are nonbinding. It investigates complaints, issues policy recommendations, trains local officials, and conducts education campaigns. NGOs asserted the NHRC was under-resourced and was not independent of the Office of the President. As of June, 5,701 allegations of human rights violations were filed with the NHRC, and it processed 4,643. There were no reported cases involving the NSL or conscientious objectors.

Ombudsman activities are the responsibility of the independent Anticorruption and Civil Rights Commission, which had adequate resources. It issued annual reports and interacted with various government institutions, including the Office of the President, the National Assembly, and ministries. The commission continued to address complaints and concerns from both citizens and foreign residents, and observers stated it generally enjoyed the public's trust.

Section 6. Discrimination, Societal Abuses, and Trafficking in Persons

Women

Rape and Domestic Violence: The law criminalizes rape and domestic violence. The police generally respond promptly and appropriately to reported incidents, and the judicial system effectively enforced the law.

Although no specific statute defines spousal rape as illegal, the Supreme Court acknowledged marital rape as illegal. The penalty for rape ranges from a minimum of three years' to life imprisonment depending on the specific circumstances. Authorities effectively investigated and prosecuted rape, although in some cases victims dropped charges against perpetrators after reaching a financial settlement with the alleged perpetrator.

The law defines domestic violence as a serious crime and authorizes authorities to order offenders to stay away from victims for up to six months. This order may be extended up to two years. Offenders may be sentenced to a maximum of five years in prison and fined up to seven million won ($6,030) for domestic violence offenses. Noncompliance with domestic violence restraining orders may result in a maximum sentence of two years in prison and a fine of up to 20 million won ($17,230). Authorities may also place offenders on probation or order them to see court-designated counselors.

When there is a danger of domestic violence recurring and an immediate need for protection, the law allows a provisional order to be issued ex officio or at the victim's request. This may restrict the subject of the order from living in the same home, approaching within 109 yards of the victim, or contacting the victim through telecommunication devices.

Domestic violence occurred in 45.6 percent of all families, according to 2015 statistics (the most recent available) from the Ministry of Gender Equality and Family. The Women's Human Rights Commission reported a higher 53.3 percent. According to an August report by the Women's Human Rights Commission of Korea, the number of domestic violence cases reported to the emergency hotline for violence against women in 2015 increased by 15.6 percent from the same period in 2014. The number of cases of reported violence in nonmarital relationships increased by 31.7 percent.

Approximately 21,270 registered couples had a foreign spouse, 69 percent of whom were foreign wives. A government-funded emergency call center for multicultural families received more than 17,950 calls pertaining to domestic violence, among which 266 callers requested assistance with transferring to a shelter.

The Ministry of Gender Equality and Family funded integrated support centers for victims of sexual violence called "sunflower centers," providing counseling, medical care and therapy, case investigations, and legal assistance. As of July, there were 36 "sunflower centers" and 100 smaller counseling centers nationwide. Other government-subsidized and nonsubsidized counseling centers operated across the country. These provided victims with free medical services, legal services, support during investigations and trials, and therapy and rehabilitation programs. A number of the facilities offered specialized services for victims with disabilities. The KNPA established a 24-hour center staffed by police officers, counselors, and nurses to provide comprehensive care to victims of sexual violence. There were also protection facilities for victims of sexual violence, including for victims with disabilities and for child and juvenile victims. The government managed family protection facilities for domestic violence victims and their children over the age of 10. The government also operated protection facilities and maintained a hotline for migrant women victims of domestic violence. The government supported group home facilities, which provided counseling, job referral, and vocational training for victims. Anti-domestic violence programs took place in all elementary and secondary schools and in local and national government offices.

In January the government launched a comprehensive action plan across several ministries to prevent sexual violence. The KNPA's Sexual Violence Special Investigation Team expanded in March to become the Women and Juveniles Investigation Office, which included 240 police officers and involved 251 different police stations nationwide. In May the Ministry of Gender Equality and Family established new mandatory regulations in the Act on the Prevention of Sexual Violence to require central and local governments to implement preventive measures by November. District and metropolitan police agencies across the country implemented Special Measures to Ensure Women's Safety for three months from June to August in response to increasing concerns about public safety after a man who espoused misogynistic messages murdered a woman in a restroom near Gangnam Station in May. As a part of these special measures, the KNPA operated a smartphone app for reporting cases and installed additional surveillance cameras, street lamps, and emergency bells in public spaces.

The law allows judges or a Ministry of Justice committee to sentence repeat sex offenders to chemical castration. Ten chemical castrations were performed in the first half of the year.

Sexual Harassment: The law obligates companies and organizations to take preventive measures against sexual harassment, and the government generally enforced the law effectively (see section 7.d.). The KNPA classifies sexual harassment as "indecent acts by compulsion." There were numerous cases of sexual harassment reported in the media throughout the year.

Civil remedies are generally available for sexual harassment claims, and education about sexual harassment was widely available nationwide. Administrative remedies at public institutions are also available.

Reproductive Rights: The law allows couples and individuals to decide freely the number, spacing, and timing of their children, manage their reproductive health, and have access to the information and means to do so, free from discrimination, coercion, and violence. Contraception and maternal health services, including skilled attendance during childbirth, emergency health care, including services for the management of complications arising from abortion, prenatal care, and essential obstetric and postpartum care, were widely accessible and available.

Discrimination: Women enjoy the same legal rights under the constitution as men. The law provides for equal pay for equal work, but the latest data from the Organization for Economic Cooperation and Development (OECD) showed the gender pay gap was 36.6 percent in 2014 (see section 7.d.). The law permits a woman to head a household, recognizes a wife's right to a portion of a couple's property, and allows a woman to maintain contact with her children after a divorce. Custody cases were decided on their merits, with women often gaining custody. The law also allows a remarried woman to change the family name of her children to her new husband's name.

Children

Birth Registration: Citizenship requires one parent be a citizen at the time of birth. Authorities also grant citizenship in circumstances where parentage is unclear or if the child would otherwise be stateless. Parents go to a district office to register their children's births. The law requires all children to be registered in family registries and prohibits adoption of children for the first week after birth.

In May the Ministry of Justice revised the family registration act to allow local governments to register children whose parents refused or failed to do so. The revised law, designed to improve the accuracy of family registers and extend protection and benefits to children who would be otherwise unregistered, came into effect in November.

Child Abuse: The law criminalizes serious injury and repeated abuse of children, provides prison terms of between five years and life, and no longer allows for suspended sentences in cases resulting in death. In 2015 the Ministry for Health and Welfare reported a 16.8 percent increase in child abuses cases compared to 2014. The number of reported abuse cases in orphanages and other child welfare facilities nearly doubled, from 180 in 2014 to 331 in 2015. The ministry operated 60 facilities and 53 shelters to treat and protect victims of child abuse and ran programs for families designed to prevent reoccurrence. The government established a 24-hour online counseling center for victims of child abuse.

Several cases of severe child abuse were reported in the media during the year, including high-profile child murder cases in January, February, and March. In August a man and woman received sentences of 30 years and 20 years in prison, respectively, for beating their seven-year-old son to death. Police investigation revealed the couple also abused their daughter and had stored the son's corpse in the refrigerator since his death in October 2012.

Early and Forced Marriage: The minimum legal age for men and women to marry is 18. There were no reported cases of forced marriage.

Sexual Exploitation of Children: The age of consent is 13. It is illegal to deceive or pressure anyone under 19 into having sexual intercourse. Children, however, were vulnerable to sex trafficking and commercial sexual exploitation through online recruitment. Some runaway girls, in particular, were subjected to sex trafficking.

The penalty for rape of a minor under age 13 ranges from 10 years to life in prison; the penalty for rape of a minor age 13 to 19 is five years to life. Other penalties include electronic monitoring of offenders, public release of their personal information, and reversible hormonal treatment (chemical castration).

The law prohibits child pornography. Offenders who produce or possess it for the purpose of selling, renting, or distributing it for profit are subject to a maximum of seven years' imprisonment. In addition, any possessor of child pornography may be fined up to 20 million won ($17,230).

The KNPA reported that cases of sexual violence committed against children decreased slightly, from 1,161 in 2014 to 1,118 in 2015.

The Ministry of Gender Equality and Family maintained centers that provided counseling, treatment, and legal assistance to child victims of sexual violence.

International Child Abductions: The country is a party to the 1980 Hague Convention on the Civil Aspects of International Child Abduction. See the Department of State's *Annual Report on International Parental Child Abduction* at travel.state.gov/content/childabduction/en/legal/compliance.html.

Anti-Semitism

The country has a small Jewish population consisting almost entirely of expatriates. There were no reports of anti-Semitic acts.

Trafficking in Persons

See the Department of State's *Trafficking in Persons Report* at www.state.gov/j/tip/rls/tiprpt/.

Persons with Disabilities

The law prohibits discrimination against persons with physical, sensory, intellectual, and mental disabilities in employment, education, air travel and other transportation, access to health care, the judicial system, or the provision of other state services. An "Act on Guarantee of Rights and Support for Developmentally Disabled Persons" went into force in November 2015 and created a special task force of prosecutors and police trained to work with persons with disabilities and their families in police investigations. The government implemented laws and programs to facilitate access to buildings, information, and communications for persons with disabilities. Many local government ordinances and regulations still directly discriminate against persons with disabilities, especially those with intellectual and mental disabilities, according to media reports and NGOs. The

National Human Rights Commission reported 512 discrimination cases against persons with disabilities in the first half of the year.

The law establishes penalties for deliberate discrimination of up to three years in prison and a fine of 30 million won ($25,840). The Ministry of Health and Welfare continued to implement a comprehensive set of policies that included encouraging public and private buildings and facilities to provide barrier-free access, providing part time employment, and employing a task force to introduce a long-term care system. The government operated rehabilitation hospitals in six regions and a national rehabilitation research center to increase opportunities and access for persons with disabilities.

The rate of involuntary commitment to a mental institution was unusually high. In 2013, 75.9 percent of commitments were involuntary, and among these, 63.5 percent were by family members. In May the Mental Health Act was revised following a Constitutional Court ruling in January that the legal provisions for involuntary institutionalization were unconstitutional. Previously, a person could be hospitalized involuntarily with the consent of two guardians and the advice of a neuropsychiatrist. The revision now requires the consent of two psychiatrists.

In August a man with intellectual disabilities was reunited with his family after 19 years of forced labor on a cattle farm less than 10 miles from his home. Ko Young-soo first arrived at the farm after being lured there by a cattle trader; he lived in a windowless storage room and received no wages for 19 years. Police found Ko when he escaped to a nearby factory in July. The couple operating the farm was indicted on criminal charges and faced prison sentences of up to 15 years. In an effort to prevent additional cases of forced labor, North Chungcheong province investigated the whereabouts of 13,776 individuals with registered intellectual disabilities. They were unable to locate 10 individuals and received 17 reports of suspected forced labor; all 27 cases were forwarded to the police.

The government provided a pension system for registered adults and children with disabilities, an allowance for children with disabilities under age 18 whose household income was below or near the National Basic Livelihood Security Standard, and a disability allowance for low-income persons age 18 and older with mild disabilities. The National Pension Service determines the degree of the disability, and local governments provide the pension directly to qualified persons. Some NGOs noted the pension and allowance system for persons with disabilities put an undue burden on families and assumed wealthier families would support their relatives with disabilities.

Children with disabilities qualified as special education beneficiaries and there was a separate system of public special education schools for children from age three to 17. Children with more significant disabilities may receive hospitalized education. All public and private schools, childcare centers, educational facilities, and training institutions must provide equipment and other resources to accommodate students with disabilities. For example, schools assigned teacher's aides to ensure children with disabilities could participate in outdoor activities.

The KNPA reported a sharp increase in the number of reports of sexual violence committed against persons with disabilities. They attribute this trend to increasing public awareness of and attention to the rights of disabled individuals following a popular film dealing with the subject and several high-profile cases of abuse publicized in the media.

National/Racial/Ethnic Minorities

As of July, more than 2.18 million foreigners (including an estimated 200,000 undocumented migrants) lived in the country, which otherwise had a racially homogeneous population of approximately 50 million. The country lacks a comprehensive antidiscrimination law, and the UN Special Rapporteur on Racism called for legislation to curb racism and xenophobia.

Societal discrimination against ethnic and racial minorities was common but under-reported. As of June, the NHRC had investigated 10 cases of alleged ethnic and racial discrimination. A poll by the Gyeonggi Institute of Research and Policy Development for Migrants' Human Rights found that of the 560 foreign workers from 17 countries who were surveyed, 43.7 percent experienced discrimination most commonly at work, 27 percent on the streets, and 18 percent at restaurants and stores.

In February a bar with a sign stating only Korean customers were allowed refused entry to a foreign woman. Although this was not perceived to be a general trend, businesses--mostly bars and nightclubs--across the country had similar overtly racist signs. Representatives of the bar in question claimed they refused to provide service to foreigners because they have no English-speaking staff, but still refused entry to the woman when she clarified she could speak Korean.

In July a middle-aged man beat a Burmese laborer in public at a subway station in Gyeonggi Province. Striking the Burmese man on the face several times, the

Korean demanded he get on his knees to apologize for having used informal speech to say, "what," when they bumped shoulders.

The NHRC reported in March that children of immigrants suffered from discrimination and lack of access to social resources. A child with cerebral palsy was found ineligible for social and medical benefits because, as a nonnational, the government did not recognize his disability. Children of non-Korean ethnicity or multiple ethnicities also experienced bullying because of their physical appearance.

In response to the steady growth of ethnic minorities due largely to the increasing number of migrant workers and foreign brides, the Ministries of Gender Equality and Family and of Employment and Labor continued programs to increase public awareness of cultural diversity and to assist foreign workers, wives, and multicultural families to adjust to life in the country. The government continued to operate foreign worker help centers across the country (see section 7.e.).

Acts of Violence, Discrimination, and Other Abuses Based on Sexual Orientation and Gender Identity

The Ministry of Justice reported the constitution's equality principles apply to LGBTI persons. The law that established the NHRC prohibits discrimination based on sexual orientation and authorizes the NHRC to review cases of such discrimination, but the law does not specify discrimination based on gender identity.

No laws either specify punishment for persons found to discriminate against LGBTI persons or provide for remedies to victims of discrimination or violence. During the first half of the year, the NHRC reported two cases of such alleged discrimination.

While there were no known cases of violence against LGBTI persons, LGBTI individuals and organizations continued to face societal discrimination. The Military Criminal Act's "disgraceful conduct" clause criminalizes consensual sodomy between men in the military with up to two years' imprisonment; in July the Constitutional Court ruled that the clause was constitutional.

The Korea Queer Culture Festival in June attracted more than 50,000 attendees, a record. It was held under heavy security without incident, but anti-LGBTI protesters staged a counter protest on the perimeter of the event's parade.

LGBTI individuals generally kept a low profile because same-sex relationships were not widely accepted, although a few entertainers were openly gay, appearing frequently on popular television programs and operating several successful businesses. Some prominent societal figures, such as student council presidents, lawyers, and human rights leaders openly acknowledged their sexual orientation. In March professors of prominent local universities launched a research group on social prejudice against LGBTI individuals.

HIV and AIDS Social Stigma

Observers claimed persons with HIV/AIDS continued to suffer from societal discrimination and social stigma. The law protects the right to confidentiality of persons with HIV/AIDS and prohibits discrimination against them.

The Ministry of Health and Welfare reported that under the Prevention of Acquired Immune Deficiency Syndrome Act, foreigners who wish to engage in teaching, entertainment, sports, or other show business and who stay in the country for more than 90 days must take a test to prove they are not HIV positive to qualify for an E (work) visa.

Section 7. Worker Rights

a. Freedom of Association and the Right to Collective Bargaining

The law provides for the right of workers to form and join independent unions, conduct legal strikes, and bargain collectively, but certain limitations apply to public officials and teachers. By law public officials may not perform a "collective act for any labor campaign." There is an exception for those who have a union-related job. A 2015 Supreme Court decision affirmed the right of all migrant workers, including undocumented workers, to form or join a union.

The law places some restrictions on unions' ability to organize their administration, including restricting the ability of union leaders to receive pay for time spent on union work. Laws banning education workers from engaging in certain political activities, such as joining a political party or openly endorsing a political party or candidate, also constrained unions' abilities to advocate for their positions. The law also prohibits dismissed workers from being union members.

The law limits the right to strike, in particular for workers in "essential services." Essential services are defined broadly and include services such as railroads, air transport, communications, water supply and other utilities, and hospitals. By law unions in essential service industries may be required to maintain 50 percent service. Individuals designated as essential by management, with input from labor unions, may not strike. The law also prohibits strikes by national and local government officials, with some exceptions for specified public servants.

By law unions must submit a request for mediation to the National Labor Relations Commission (NLRC) before a strike; otherwise, the strike is illegal. In most cases, mediation must be completed within 10 days. Strikes initiated following this period are legal if they obtain majority support from union membership. The law prohibits strikes when a dispute is referred to binding arbitration.

The law adopts a narrow interpretation of "labor dispute," which makes strikes on many issues falling under managerial control, such as downsizing and layoffs, illegal. Strikes not specifically pertaining to labor conditions, wages, benefits, or working hours are also considered illegal. Stakeholders noted that in practice strike procedures were overly burdensome.

The law permits workers to file complaints of unfair labor practices against employers who interfere with union organizing or who discriminate against union members. The NLRC may require employers to reinstate workers fired for union activities. The law prohibits retribution against workers who conduct a legal strike. Labor organizations noted the inability of full-time labor union officials to receive wages and onerous registration requirements for individuals involved in bargaining effectively limited legal protections against unfair labor practices.

The government generally enforced legislation related to freedom of association and collective bargaining. Employers who violate a regulation on unfair labor practices may be imprisoned for a maximum of two years or fined up to 20 million won ($17,230). In addition, an employer can be punished for disregarding a NLRC order to reinstate a worker. The law sets penalties against employers who refuse or neglect to accept unions' legitimate requests for bargaining (maximum of two years' imprisonment or a penalty of up to 20 million won ($17,230) or conduct lockouts (maximum of one year in prison or a penalty of up to 10 million won ($8,610)). The law also penalizes illegal strike activities with imprisonment for up to five years or a fine of up to 50 million won ($43,070), depending on the offense.

Many labor organizations generally operated without government interference; however, stakeholders noted the government used overly broad criminal legal provisions, including the "obstruction of business" provisions, to justify criminal prosecutions and other extreme measures against union leaders to suppress strikes. In his June report, the UN Special Rapporteur on the rights to freedom of peaceful assembly and of association highlighted a number of concerns regarding interference with independence and operations of unions, including by employers.

Following a November 2015 "People's Rally" (see section 1.d.) organized by the Korean Confederation of Trade Unions, union president Han Sang-gyun was sentenced in July to five years in prison and a 500,000 won ($430) fine on six mostly obstruction-related charges. The court also held Han personally responsible for injuries to 76 Korean National Police personnel, obstruction of public duty of 32 police personnel, and damage to 43 police buses and 138 pieces of equipment, including torn police uniforms and vests. Han was one of six labor unionists still in police custody as of October in the aftermath of the rally, which gathered more than 64,000 protesters.

NGOs and labor experts noted a one-year sentence had been the norm in recent years for leading labor protests, and progressive local media noted Han's punishment was "the stiffest sentence for a rally organizer since the country's democratization in 1987." The UN Special Rapporteur on the rights to freedom of peaceful assembly and of association expressed his concern about "a trend of gradual regression on the rights to freedom of peaceful assembly and of association," during his January visit.

In his June report, the UN Special Rapporteur on the rights to freedom of peaceful assembly and of association noted examples of antiunion practices by companies, including: encouraging the formation of management-supported unions; undermining employee unions through various means including surveillance, threats, and undue pressure on members; disguised subcontracting to avoid selected employer responsibilities and dismissal of members; firing union leaders and workers following strike action; and assigning union leaders demeaning jobs to demoralize them. He noted employers allegedly used labor relations consultancy firms to obtain advice that facilitates the erosion of trade union rights. The International Trade Union Confederation noted similar concerns during the year, including employers imposing the choice of union on construction workers and discrimination against unionized workers at a car factory.

As of September, the Migrants' Trade Union (MTU) had approximately 1,200 members. In its first year as a recognized union, the MTU conducted organizing campaigns and training for workers. It also mobilized members to advocate for a minimum wage increase and better working conditions. Nonetheless, undocumented foreign workers still face difficulties participating in union activities due to fear of exposing themselves to arrest and deportation.

b. Prohibition of Forced or Compulsory Labor

The law prohibits all forms of forced or compulsory labor.

The government generally enforced the law effectively. Penalties for trafficking in persons, including for forced labor, are commensurate with those for other serious crimes. The criminal code prohibits all forms of trafficking and prescribes up to 15 years' imprisonment for trafficking crimes. In August a couple was indicted for forcing an intellectually disabled man to work at a cattle farm for no wages and under harsh conditions for 19 years (see section 6, "Persons with Disabilities").

There were reports some workers were subject to forced labor. Migrant workers who traveled to the country for employment sometimes incurred thousands of dollars in debts, making them vulnerable to debt bondage. Some migrant workers in the agriculture, livestock, and fishing industries faced conditions indicative of forced labor, including deceptive recruiting practices, confiscation of passports, and nonpayment of wages.

The Ministry of Employment and Labor (MOEL) reported passport confiscation was "rare" due to increased employer awareness that it is a violation of the Immigration Control Law. Civil society groups and foreign workers centers explained that, although illegal confiscation was increasingly uncommon, many foreign workers unknowingly sign paperwork legally authorizing employers to obtain passports and other forms of identification on their behalf; thus, many of the problems associated with passport confiscation remain unaddressed.

Amnesty International's 2015/16 report noted it was extremely difficult for migrant workers to seek alternative employment under the terms of the Employment Permit System even if they experienced exploitation or abuse by their employer and highlighted poor conditions for migrant workers in agriculture (see section 7.d.), including conditions indicative of forced labor.

Also see the Department of State's *Trafficking in Persons Report* at www.state.gov/j/tip/rls/tiprpt/.

c. Prohibition of Child Labor and Minimum Age for Employment

The law prohibits the employment of persons under age 15 without an authorization certificate from the MOEL. Authorities issued few such certificates for full-time employment because education is compulsory through middle school (approximately age 15). To obtain employment, children under 18 must obtain written approval from either parents or guardians. Employers must limit minors' overtime hours and may not employ minors at night without special permission from the ministry. According to labor laws, employers in industries considered harmful or hazardous in ethical or health terms are prohibited from employing children under 18 and can face fines of up to 20 million won ($17,230) or three years' imprisonment. The government inspects businesses employing large numbers of juveniles.

There were some reports of commercial sexual exploitation of children (see section 6, "Children").

d. Discrimination with Respect to Employment and Occupation

The constitution and laws prohibit discrimination in employment based on race, gender, disability, sexual orientation, and social status. The law states there shall be no discrimination in economic, social, or cultural life based on sex, religion, or social status. Labor laws generally provide foreign and migrant workers the same legal protections as nationals. The law explicitly prohibits employment discrimination on the basis of gender, age, religion, physical condition, social status, hometown, education, marital status, pregnancy, nationality, or medical history. There are no laws explicitly prohibiting discrimination on the basis of color, political opinion, language, or HIV or other communicable disease status.

The law requires equal pay for equal work when men and women do work of equal value in the same business.

Any business with 50 or more full-time employees is required to meet an employment quota for persons with disabilities (3 percent for government agencies, 2.3 percent to 3 percent for public organizations, and 2.3 percent for private companies). Foreign companies operating in export processing zones are exempt from this requirement.

There was no comprehensive mechanism to enforce all these provisions if discrimination occurred. The law establishes penalties of up to 30 million won ($25,840) and five years' imprisonment for the chief executive officers of companies that fire women during pregnancy or immediately after giving birth, and up to 10 million won ($8,610) and two years' imprisonment for failure to provide paid maternity leave. The law provides a fine of up to five million won ($4,310) for companies found guilty of practicing sexual discrimination against women in hiring and promotions. Business owners are subject to a penalty of up to 10 million won ($8,610) for an incident of sexual harassment in the workplace, but harassment itself is not a criminal act.

Any private company or public organization with 30 to 100 full time workers that does not meet its quota for hiring persons with disabilities is subject to a monthly penalty ranging from 710,000 to 1.166 million won ($612 to $1005) for each available qualified person with a disability whom it fails to hire. An additional penalty may be imposed if the employment rate of workers with disabilities does not reach 50 percent of the required quota.

Discrimination occurred against persons with HIV/AIDs, women, persons with disabilities and migrant workers. HIV discrimination continued for foreigners seeking certain kinds of work.

Discrimination against women in both hiring and in employment continued. Women continued to experience a pay gap, and a higher percentage of women filled lower-paying, low skilled, contract jobs. According to MOEL, approximately 25,000 mothers could not get paid maternity leave and stopped working in 2015. Women often faced difficulties returning to the workforce after childbirth. Under the Labor Standards Act, an employer that fires an employee during pregnancy or within three months of giving birth is subject to a fine of up to 30 million won ($25,500), with the company's executive officer facing up to five years in prison. Denial of maternity leave could result in a 10 million won ($8,500) fine and two years of imprisonment. Enforcement of these laws remained a challenge, and the Ministry of Gender Equality and Family (MOGEF) launched a Smart Labor Surveillance program to track compliance with family leave policies and strengthen supervision of workplaces that violate leave regulations.

Nationwide there were 150 New Work for Women Centers that provided employment support and vocational training for women. As of September, more than 287,000 women requested assistance from MOGEF in finding employment; among them, 11,000 received vocational training. More than 112,000 women subsequently obtained jobs after receiving training or other assistance from the ministry. MOEL maintained an affirmative action program for public institutions with 50 or more employees and private institutions with 500 or more employees. The program requires these institutions to comply with a hiring plan devised by the ministry if they do not maintain a female workforce greater than or equal to 60 percent of the ratio of female workers compared with total workers in relevant occupations. When the Public Procurement Service evaluates submitted bids, it gives more weight to businesses with effective affirmative action measures.

MOEL reported the number of women in entry-level civil service positions and diplomatic positions continued to increase. The Korean Employers Federation reported a slight increase in the number of female managers in businesses with more than 1,000 workers. A September survey conducted by CEO Score reported, however, that there were no female executives at any of the country's 30 public enterprises.

The MOEL reported 164 cases of sexual harassment in the workplace between January and June. Approximately 16,000 administrative agencies, local governments, and public organizations are obligated to submit annual plans and ratings to the Ministry of Gender Equality and Family on efforts to prevent sexual harassment in the workplace and raise awareness. The Ministry of Gender Equality and Family also conducts field inspections and requires additional training for offices that rate poorly on preventive policies.

The Minimum Wage Act excludes "those who clearly lack the capacity to work." In 2014 the UN Committee on the Rights of Persons with Disabilities stated its concern that many persons with disabilities who work, especially those with psychosocial disabilities, received compensation below the minimum wage. In May the Ministry of Employment and Labor publicized a list of 633 firms that did not meet quotas for employing persons with disabilities. A person with disabilities working for any company with 50 full time employees can request a reasonable accommodation, such as adjusted working hours, and the denial of such a request could constitute discrimination. According to the Korea Employment Agency for the Disabled's latest report, approximately one-half of the estimated 1.39 million persons between ages 15 to 64 with disabilities were employed.

NGOs and the local media reported irregular workers were at greater risk for discrimination because of their status (see section 7.e.).

Many migrant workers face discrimination and difficult working conditions. The maximum length of stay under the Employment Permit System (EPS) is four years and 10 months, just under the five years needed to apply for permanent residency. Some NGOs and civil society groups asserted this explicitly excludes foreign workers from permanent residence or citizenship eligibility. Amnesty

International's 2015-16 report stated the terms of the EPS make it extremely difficult for migrant workers to seek alternative employment even if they experience exploitation or abuse by their employer (see sections 7.b and 7.e.).

The law prohibits discrimination against informal or irregular workers (those who do not have full-time, permanent employment and who do not receive benefits at the same level as permanent workers) and requires the conversion of those employed longer than two years to permanent status. Nonetheless, subcontracted workers (known as "dispatched workers") and temporary workers comprised approximately one-fifth of wage workers in the labor force and faced discriminatory working conditions. The law prohibits unfavorable treatment in wages, working conditions, or benefits on the grounds of employment type, but discrimination persisted in practice.

Both labor and business groups complained the two-year conversion provision prompted many businesses to limit the contract terms of irregular workers and accept the cost of bringing in new workers rather than bear the extra costs of permanent employees. NGOs and the local media reported irregular workers were at greater risk for discrimination because of their status.

e. Acceptable Conditions of Work

The annual national minimum wage was 6,030 won ($5.20) per hour. A person making the minimum wage for a 40-hour workweek would earn significantly less than the minimum monthly cost of living for a family of four, according to the Ministry of Health and Welfare. There were 2,037 violations of the Minimum Wage Act across 1,481 businesses filed with the government in 2015, the latest year for which such data were available. Minimum wage requirements do not apply to foreign workers aboard vessels weighing more than 20 tons in coastal waters.

The law requires employers to allow 30 minutes' rest in a four-hour work period and one hour's rest in an eight-hour work period. The law also allows a flexible system under which employees may work more than eight hours during certain days or more than 40 hours per week during certain weeks, so long as average weekly work hours for any given two-week period do not exceed 40. For employers who adopt a flexible system, amounts exceeding 40 hours constitute overtime. Foreign companies operating in the export processing zones are exempt from labor regulations that mandate one day of rest a week, such as weekends, also referred to as "weekly rest." Persons working in the financial/insurance industry, publicly invested companies, state corporations, and companies with more than five full time employees are required to receive premium pay at a 50 percent higher rate for work in excess of 40 hours per week. The law limits overtime of ordinary workers to 12 hours a week to protect workers' health.

The government sets occupational health and safety standards and is responsible for monitoring industry adherence. Under the law, workers have the right to remove themselves from situations of danger without jeopardizing their employment. These standards apply to all sectors, including agriculture, fisheries, or mining.

The government enforced laws on acceptable conditions of work for all sectors. Penalties for violations of occupational safety and health provisions are a maximum of seven years in prison and fines of up to 100 million won ($86,130). Penalties for violating overtime regulations are a maximum of two years in prison and fines of up to 10 million won ($8,705), while penalties for violating the minimum wage law are up to three years in prison and 20 million won ($17,409) in fines. The government conducted labor inspections both proactively, according to regulations, and reactively, within a month after an accident occurred. MOEL employed approximately 1,185 labor inspectors and 366 industrial safety inspectors in 47 offices nationwide as of September. The International Labor Organization observed, however, that the number of labor inspectors was insufficient and that unannounced inspections were rare. The Korea Occupational Safety and Health Agency conducted more than 16,647 industrial safety and welfare inspections as of August. The government also conducted educational programs to prevent accidents. During the year the government also conducted inspections of establishments employing foreign, temporary entertainment workers, a vulnerable migrant population.

According to an August OECD report, average annual working hours are very high, at 2,113 per worker.

A set of regulations outlines legal protections for migrant (those under the EPS) and foreign (all others) workers. Permit holders may work only in certain industries and had limited job mobility, but most enjoyed the same protections under labor law as citizens. Contract workers, irregular workers, and part-time workers accounted for a substantial portion of the workforce, particularly in electronics, automotive, and services sectors.

Workers under the EPS faced multiple restrictions on employment mobility. Such workers lose their legal status if they lost their job and do not find a new employer within three months. If a migrant worker is not able to get a job within three months, authorities could cancel his/her work permit, forcing the worker to return home or remain in the country illegally. This situation was particularly difficult for seasonal workers, such as those involved in agriculture or construction. Migrant workers did not have access to lists of companies that were hiring when they wanted to change jobs, which made it more difficult for these workers to change jobs freely. Employers effectively controlled the list of job-seeking workers and had the right to contact the person they choose. Migrant laborers were required to return home after a maximum of four years and 10 months in the country but could apply to reenter after three months.

To prevent violations and improve working conditions for migrant and foreign workers, the government provided pre-employment training to newly arrived foreign workers, workplace adaptation training to those who changed workplaces, and training to employers who hired foreign workers. The government funded 39 support centers for foreign workers nationwide, a call center that provided foreign workers with counseling services in 15 languages, Korean language and cultural programs, shelter, and free health-care services. MOEL continued programs for foreign workers, including free legal advice, counseling, translation services, health checkups in their native language, and the establishment of several human rights protection centers for foreigners.

The law requires severance payments, classified since 2014 as "departure guarantee insurance," to migrant workers departing the country who worked for at least one year. In April the Constitutional Court ruled that paying foreign workers' severance pay only after they depart the country does not violate the constitution. Previously, foreign workers received severance payments prior to returning to their home country. Many workers reported difficulty receiving payments after returning to their home country due to banking regulations and intransigent employers. NGOs reported that many departing migrants never received these payments.

Some NGOs reported migrant workers were particularly vulnerable to exploitation because the law excludes regulations on working hours, holidays, and benefits for the agricultural, livestock, and fisheries industries--industries with large populations of migrant workers. NGOs and foreign government officials expressed concern about the lack of cultural awareness among employers of foreign workers, citing instances when Muslim fishermen from Indonesia were continuously served pork in their meals onboard a South Korean fishing vessel. Other NGOs reported foreign laborers sometimes faced physical abuse and exploitation by employers in the form of longer working hours and lower wages than their South Korean counterparts. Moreover, according to NGOs, workers also faced unexpected contract changes, such as the deduction of accommodation or meal expenses from wages. The OECD reported that South Korean workers earn 1.55 times as much as foreign workers, a very large wage gap.

The government reported descriptions of and statistics on work-related injuries and fatalities on a quarterly basis on its websites. There were 90,129 industrial work-related accidents reported and 1,810 fatalities. In June a sulfuric acid leak at Korea Zinc Company in Ulsan led to the deaths of two workers and burn injuries for three others.